RODGERS AND HAMMERSTEIN™

PIANO SOLO

THE SOUND OF MUSIC®

FOR JAZZ PIANO

ISBN 978-1-4234-5381-9

WILLIAMSON MUSIC®

A RODGERS AND HAMMERSTEIN COMPANY

www.rnhtheatricals.com

EXCLUSIVELY DISTRIBUTED BY

HAL•LEONARD®
CORPORATION

7777 W. BLUEMOUND RD. P.O. BOX 13819 MILWAUKEE, WI 53213

Visit Hal Leonard Online at
www.halleonard.com

RODGERS AND HAMMERSTEIN™

THE SOUND OF MUSIC

FOR JAZZ PIANO

CONTENTS

THE SOUND OF MUSIC

Lyrics by OSCAR HAMMERSTEIN II
Music by RICHARD RODGERS

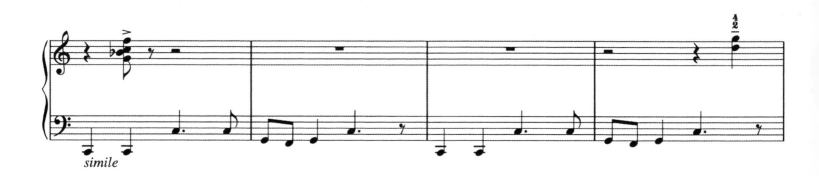

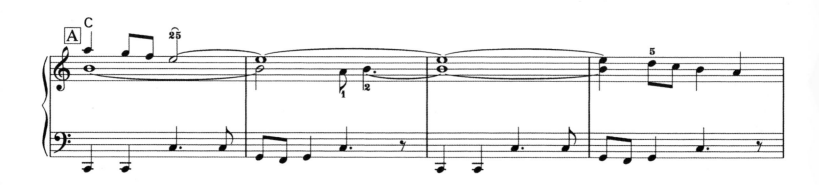

THE SOUND OF MUSIC

Lyrics by OSCAR HAMMERSTEIN II
Music by RICHARD RODGERS

MARIA

Lyrics by OSCAR HAMMERSTEIN II
Music by RICHARD RODGERS

I HAVE CONFIDENCE

Lyrics and Music by
RICHARD RODGERS

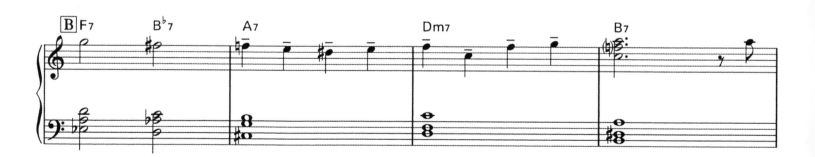

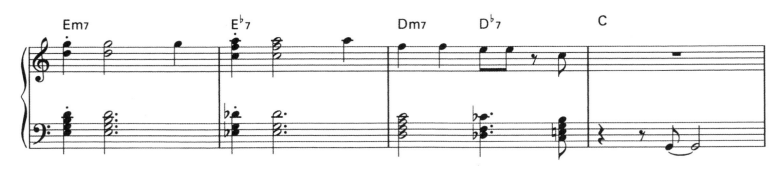

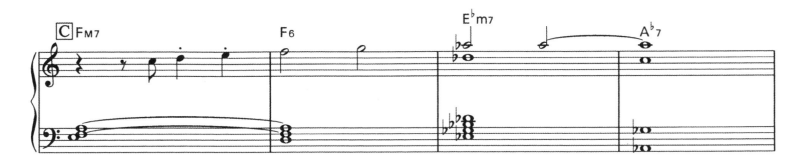

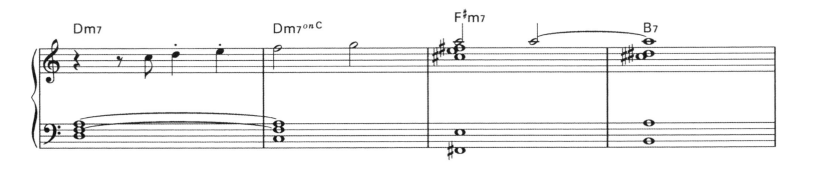

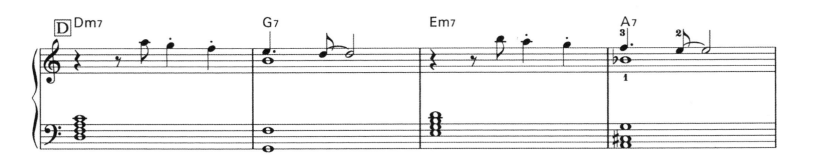

SIXTEEN GOING ON SEVENTEEN

Lyrics by OSCAR HAMMERSTEIN II
Music by RICHARD RODGERS

MY FAVORITE THINGS

Lyrics by OSCAR HAMMERSTEIN II
Music by RICHARD RODGERS

Fast groove ♩ = 200

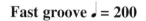

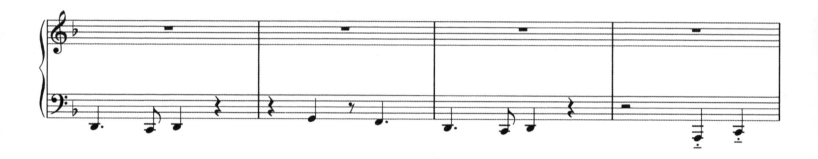

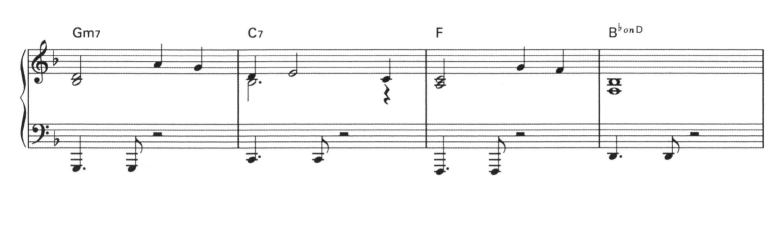

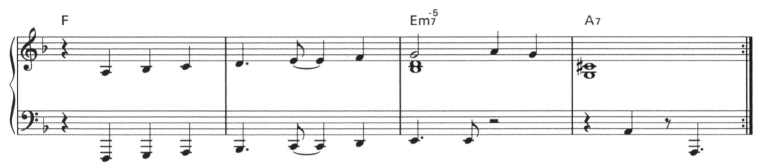

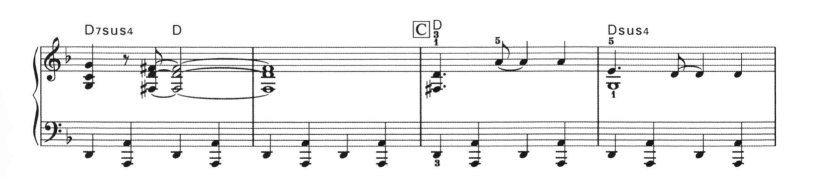

CLIMB EV'RY MOUNTAIN

Lyrics by OSCAR HAMMERSTEIN II
Music by RICHARD RODGERS

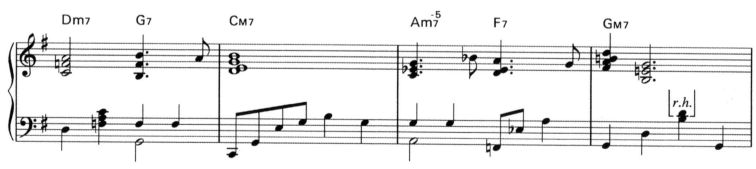

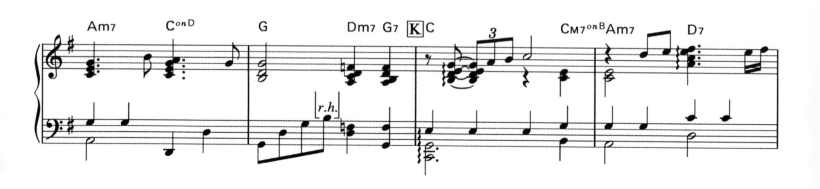

THE LONELY GOATHERD

Lyrics by OSCAR HAMMERSTEIN II
Music by RICHARD RODGERS

Very fast bounce ♩ = 200

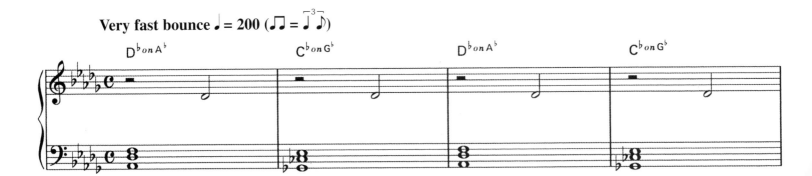

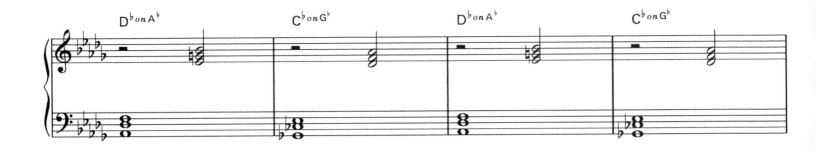

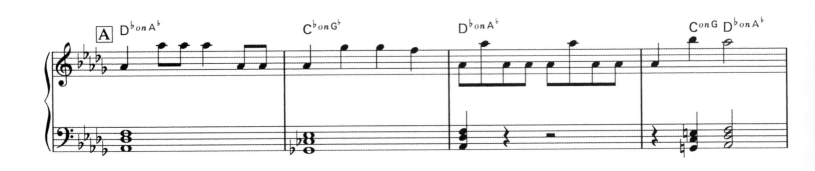

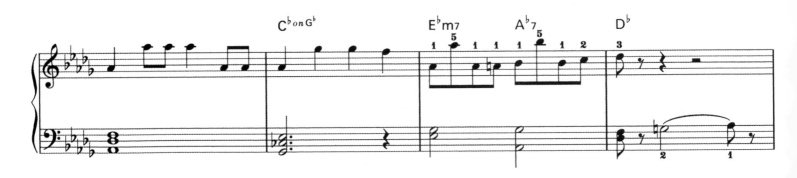

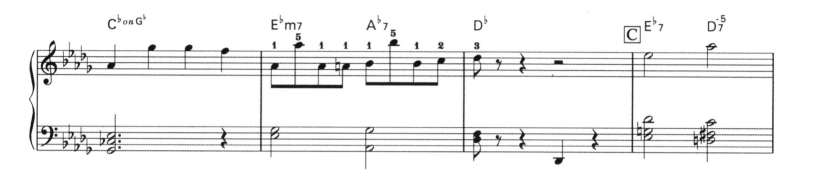

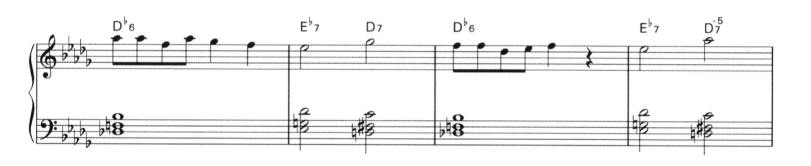

DO-RE-MI

Lyrics by OSCAR HAMMERSTEIN II
Music by RICHARD RODGERS

DO-RE-MI

Lyrics by OSCAR HAMMERSTEIN II
Music by RICHARD RODGERS

Light Swing ♩ = 168

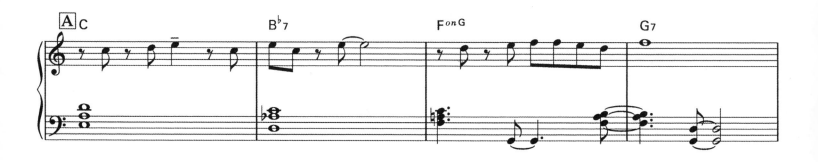

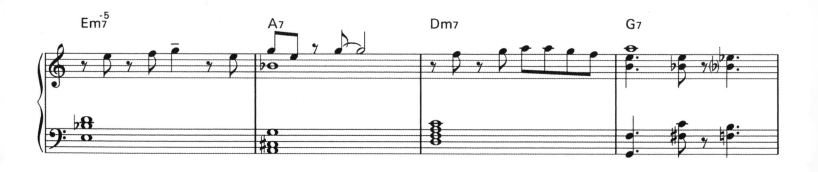

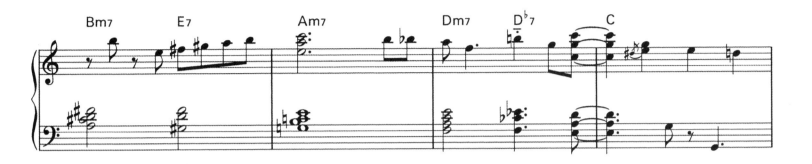

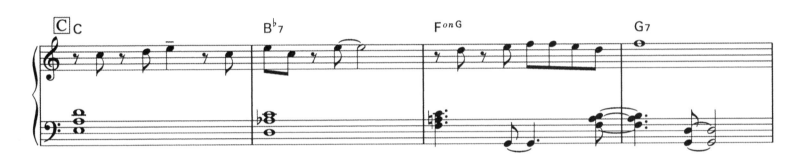

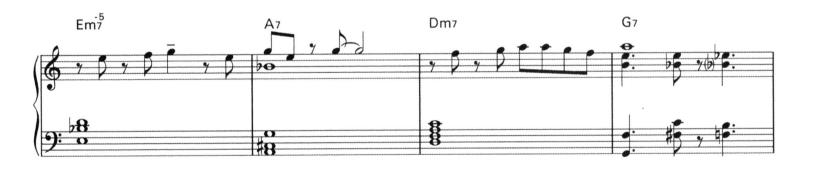

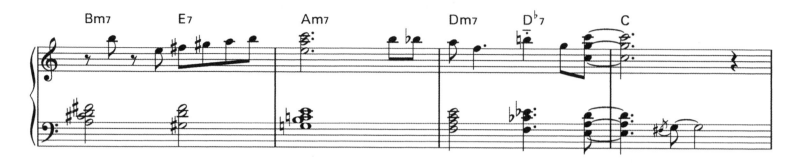

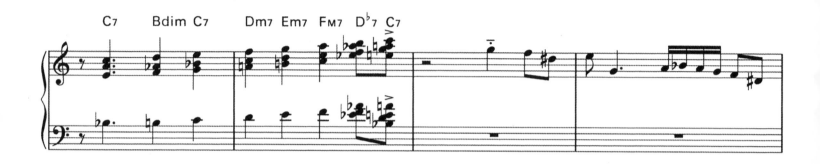

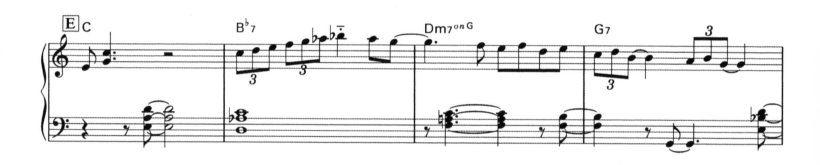

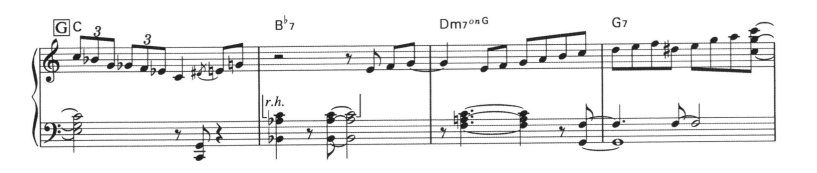

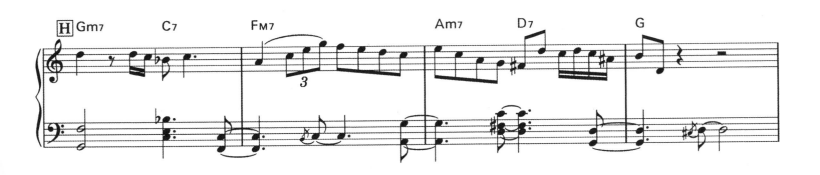

54

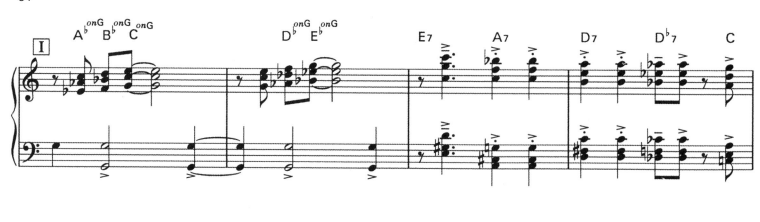

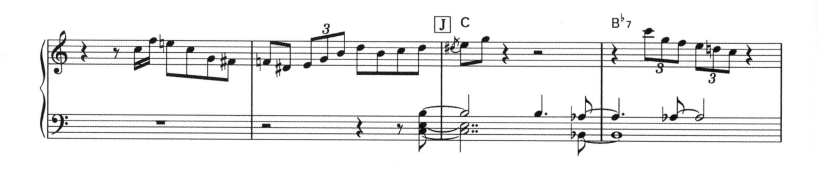

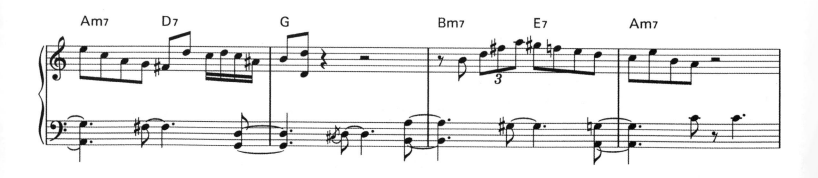

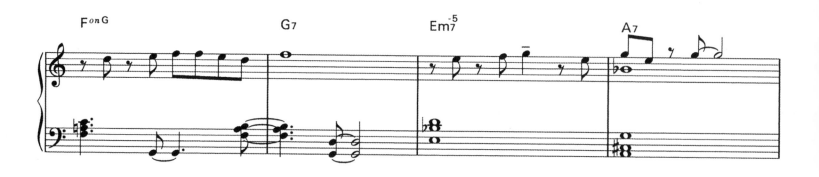

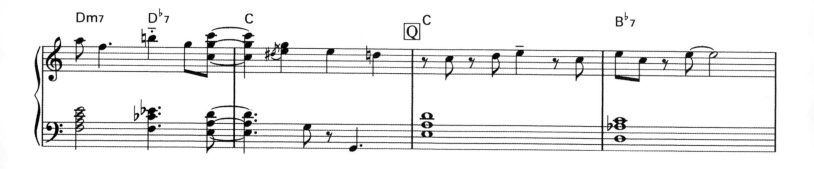

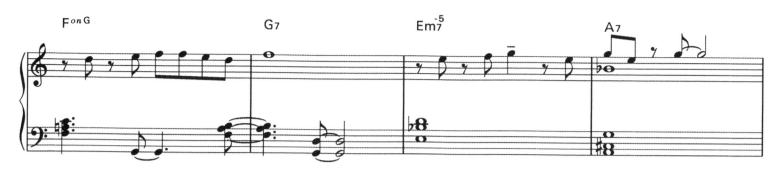

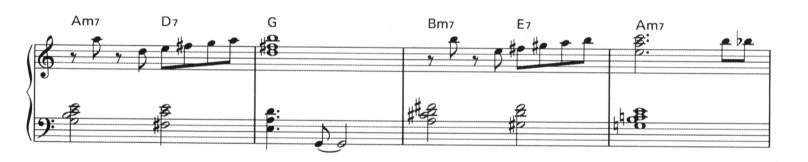

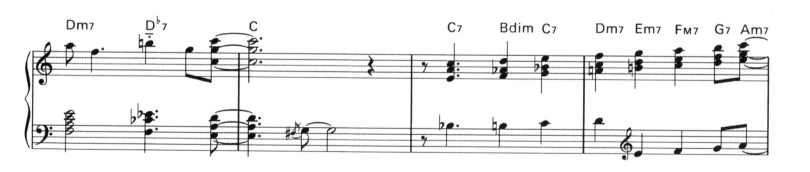

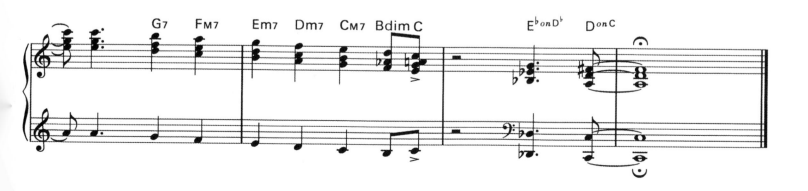

SOMETHING GOOD

Lyrics and Music by
RICHARD RODGERS

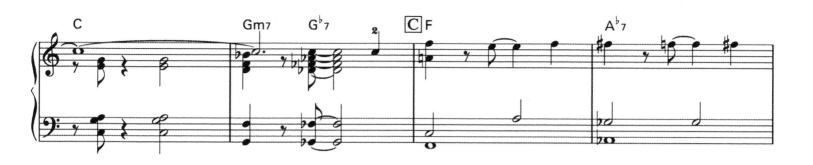

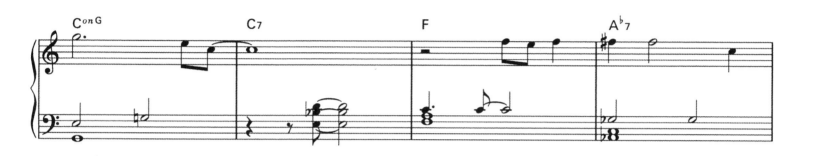

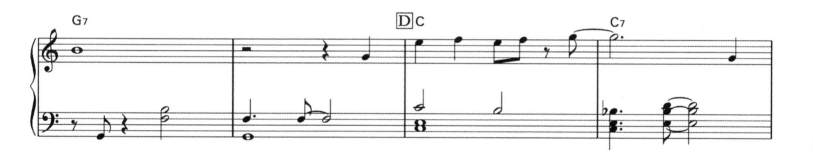

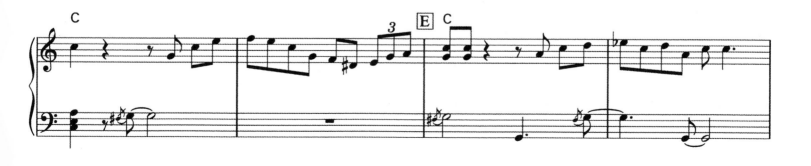

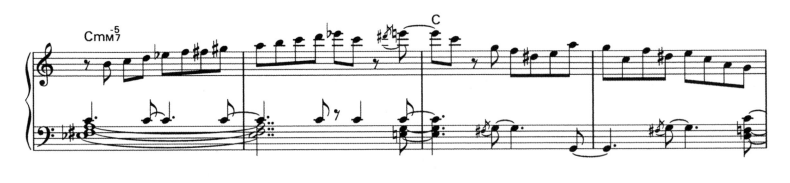

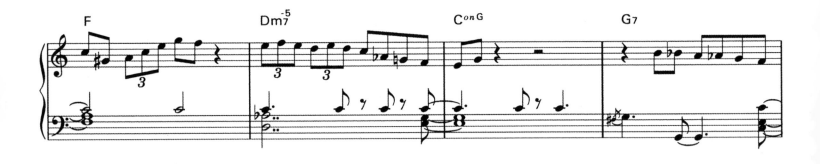

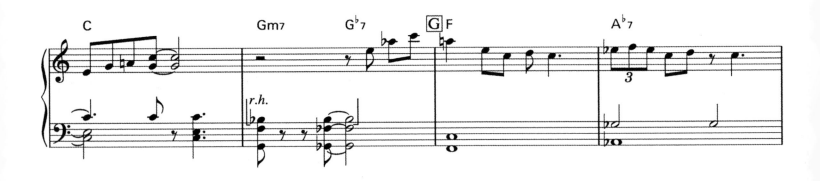

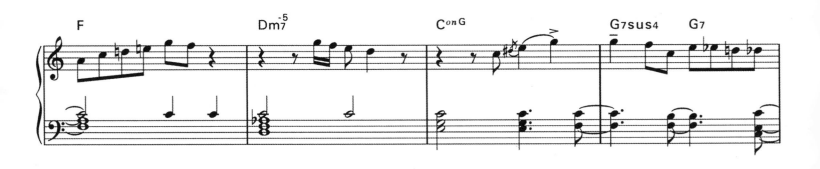

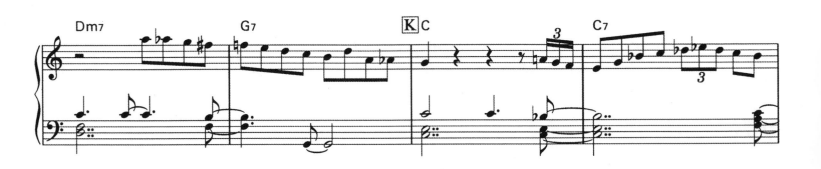

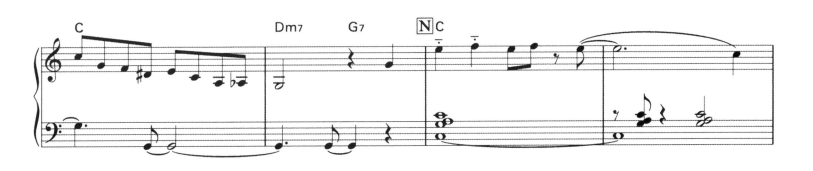

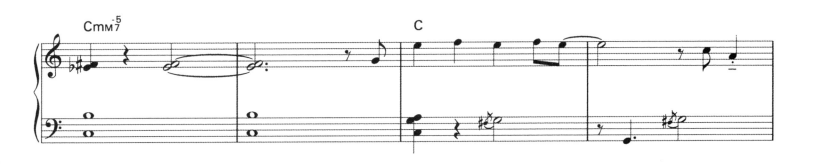

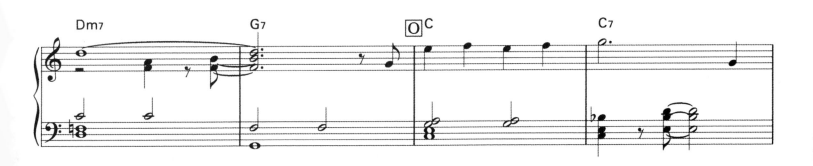

64

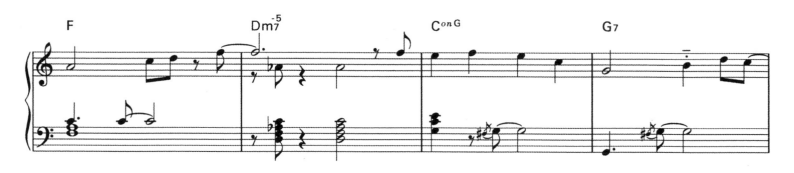

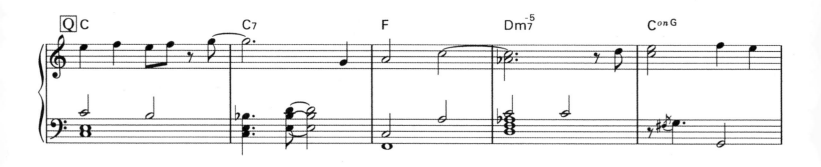

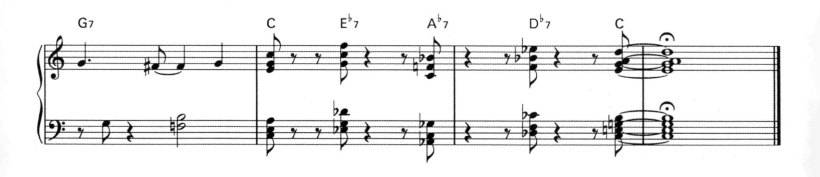

EDELWEISS

Lyrics by OSCAR HAMMERSTEIN II
Music by RICHARD RODGERS

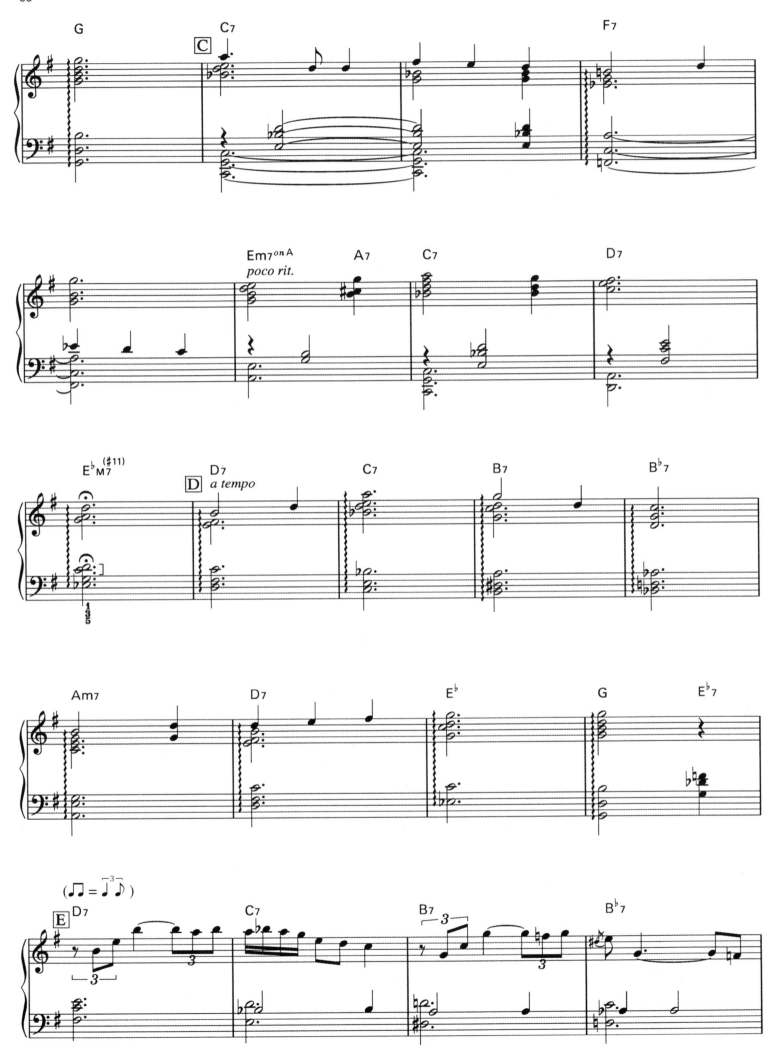

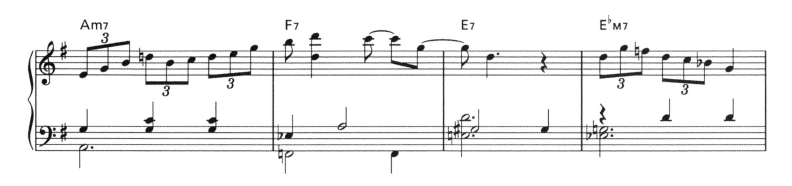

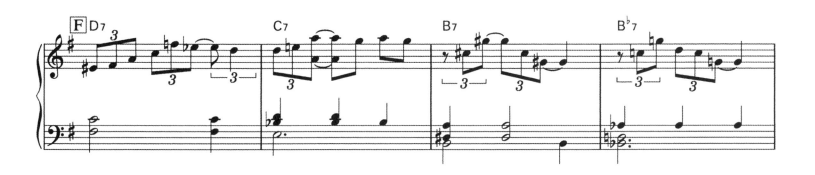

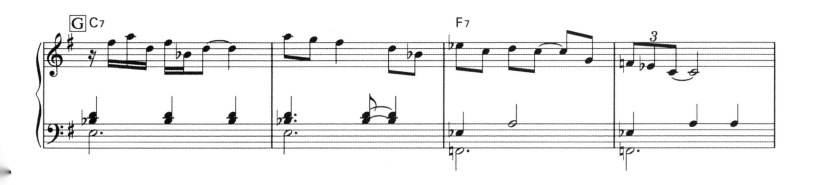

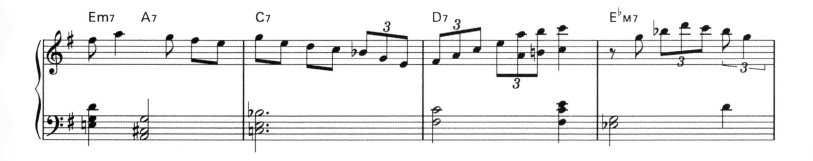

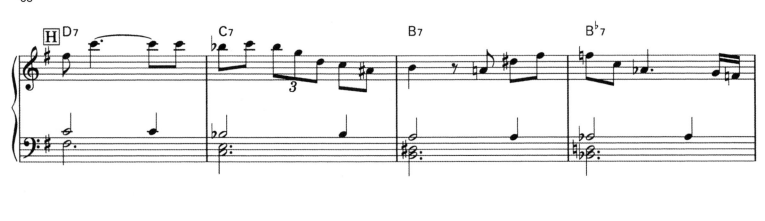

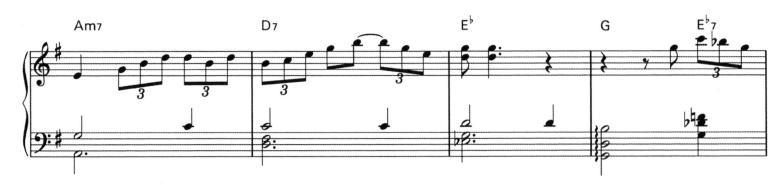

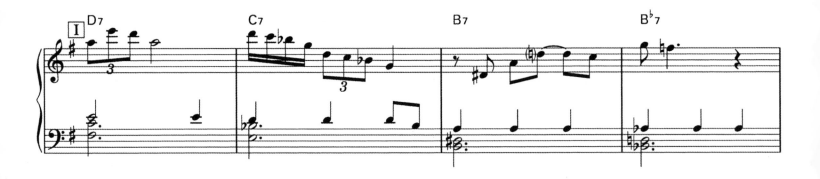

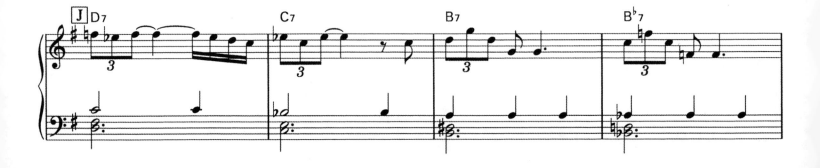

SO LONG, FAREWELL

Lyrics by OSCAR HAMMERSTEIN II
Music by RICHARD RODGERS